The
Household
Legal *and*
Financial
Document
Organizer

This book belongs to:

Name _____

Address _____

City, state, zip code _____

Phone number _____

Email address _____

The

Household
Legal *and*
Financial
Document
Organizer

Revell

a division of Baker Publishing Group
Grand Rapids, Michigan

© 2012 by Baker Publishing Group

Published by Revell
a division of Baker Publishing Group
P.O. Box 6287, Grand Rapids, MI 49516-6287
www.revellbooks.com

ISBN 978-0-8007-2019-3

Printed in China

Scripture is taken from GOD'S WORD®. © 1995 God's Word to
the Nations. Used by permission of Baker Publishing Group.

Produced with the assistance of The Livingstone Corporation
(www.LivingstoneCorp.com). Project staff includes Kelly
Barton, Linda Taylor, and Linda Washington. Articles written
by Tim Baker, Sharon Kaufman, Tom Taylor, and Emily White
Youree.

12 13 14 15 16 17 18   7 6 5 4 3 2 1

Contents

Welcome

Our lives are filled with paperwork and numbers. We have bank accounts and passwords. We have health and medical documents. We have property ownership papers, insurance papers for all that property, financial documents, end-of-life documents.

At a moment's notice, can you locate the important papers in your life? Welcome to *The Household Legal and Financial Document Organizer*. We've created this especially with you and all your many papers in mind. This is the book that will hold essential information— or the location of that information. In this handy book, we will help you:

» keep track of contact information for the professionals in your life (doctors, lawyers, accountants)
» record your basic medical and prescription information
» fill out a family tree for you and for your spouse (especially helpful for keeping track of maiden names in the family)
» list the essential documents that you have and where you keep them
» record user names and passwords for your favorite websites
» spell out your end-of-life desires
» fill the pockets with special documents that are important to you

In addition, we have included several informational articles based on research and interviews with professionals to give you a better understanding about topics such as life insurance, identity theft, what should be in your safe deposit box, and even what kinds of questions are asked at a funeral home.

Reach for this book often. Keep it up-to-date. Make sure that you record everything that pertains to you. This book is all about *you*—and there's absolutely nothing wrong with that.

In addition, if something should happen to you, your loved ones will be able to know where to find documentation about your life along with your wishes.

Above all, we hope *The Household Legal and Financial Document Organizer* gives you peace of mind.

—The Editors

How to Use the Pockets

In this book we provide you with four pockets. We don't recommend putting highly sensitive documents in the pockets; instead, use the information in the articles in this book to give you an idea of where to place those various important documents.

These pockets are for you to use to hold other items or documents that are important to you. This book will grow with you over the years, and you may update it as needed.

Suggestions:

» Use a pocket as a "smile file." Store notes from people who told you how much you mean to them.

(It's a great self-esteem boost to go back and read these from time to time.)

» Use a pocket to document your "fifteen minutes of fame"—newspaper articles where your name is featured, etc.

» Use a pocket as a temporary holding place for items such as bonds and deeds and tax forms that will be transferred to a more secure place.

» Use a pocket for favorite hymns, poems, Scripture verses, etc., that you would like read or sung at your funeral or memorial service.

Give advice to a wise person, and he will become even wiser. Teach a righteous person, and he will learn more.

Proverbs 9:9

WHO
Do I Know?

A friend always loves.
Proverbs 17:17

Essential People Locator

My Family Tree

My Spouse's Family Tree

Memorable Dates

Essential People Locator

Use these pages to record the names and contact information for all those people who are involved in your physical, spiritual, emotional, and financial life—as well as anyone else important to know, such as your closest neighbor. We have offered some categories and then given you space to add your own.

■ Emergency Contacts

Name		Name	
Email address	Phone number	Email address	Phone number
Address		Address	

Name		Name	
Email address	Phone number	Email address	Phone number
Address		Address	

■ Physicians

Name	Type of doctor	Name	Type of doctor
Email address	Phone number	Email address	Phone number
Address		Address	

Name	Type of doctor	Name	Type of doctor
Email address	Phone number	Email address	Phone number
Address		Address	

Name	Type of doctor	Name	Type of doctor
Email address	Phone number	Email address	Phone number
Address		Address	

Name	Type of doctor	Name	Type of doctor
Email address	Phone number	Email address	Phone number
Address		Address	

■ Dentist

Name

Email address | Phone number

Address

■ Pharmacist

Name

Email address | Phone number

Address

■ Optometrist

Name

Email address | Phone number

Address

■ Accountant

Name

Email address | Phone number

Address

■ Lawyers

Name

Email address | Phone number

Address

Name

Email address | Phone number

Address

■ Insurance Agents

Name

Email address | Phone number

Address

Type of insurance

Name

Email address | Phone number

Address

Type of insurance

■ Financial Advisor

Name

Email address | Phone number

Address

■ Other _____

Name

Email address | Phone number

Address

My Family Tree

My Spouse's Family Tree

Memorable Dates

Beyond birthdays and anniversaries (probably saved in other locations), you have many other special dates that are important to you—first date, date of engagement, "gotcha" dates (in the case of adopted children), graduation or retirement dates, or special ceremony dates. This is your page to record those memorable occasions.

Memorable event	Date
Why it's so important to me	

Memorable event	Date
Why it's so important to me	

Memorable event	Date
Why it's so important to me	

Memorable event	Date
Why it's so important to me	

Memorable event	Date
Why it's so important to me	

Memorable event	Date
Why it's so important to me	

Memorable event	Date
Why it's so important to me	

Memorable event	Date
Why it's so important to me	

Memorable event	Date
Why it's so important to me	

Memorable event	Date
Why it's so important to me	

WHAT
Do I Have and
WHERE
Is It Kept?

Use priceless wisdom and foresight.

Proverbs 3:21

Essential Documents

Essential Document Locator

What I Own

Important Medical Information

Choosing Life Insurance

What Should Be in a Safe Deposit Box?

Safe Deposit Box Contents

Essential Documents

The checklist below provides many possibilities for the essential documents you may have. Check all that apply. (The location of these documents will be filled out on page 18.)

■ Personal

- ☐ Driver's license
- ☐ Social security card
- ☐ Birth certificate
- ☐ Children's birth certificates
- ☐ Adoption papers
- ☐ Children's adoption papers
- ☐ Marriage license/certificate
- ☐ Prenuptial agreement
- ☐ Divorce/separation papers
- ☐ Death certificates
- ☐ Passport

- ☐ Military service/discharge papers
- ☐ Naturalization or residency papers
- ☐ Employment paperwork
- ☐ Will
- ☐ Trusts
- ☐ Living will
- ☐ Power of attorney
- ☐ Healthcare power of attorney
- ☐ Burial plot papers
- ☐ Personal loan or debt agreement

■ Possessions

- ☐ Deed for home/renter's lease
- ☐ Deed for other properties
- ☐ Mortgage paperwork
- ☐ Property tax statements
- ☐ Vehicle titles

- ☐ Vehicle registrations
- ☐ Recreational vehicle registrations (boat, motorcycle)
- ☐ Household inventory
- ☐ Appraisals of possessions
- ☐ Appraisals of property

■ Education

- ☐ Diplomas

- ☐ Transcripts

■ Insurances

- ☐ Home or renter's insurance policy
- ☐ Medical insurance policy
- ☐ Vehicle insurance policy
- ☐ Other insurance policy (boat/RV)
- ☐ Long-term care insurance policy
- ☐ Life insurance policy
- ☐ Disability insurance policy

■ Finances

- ☐ Bank statements
- ☐ Checkbook
- ☐ Savings passbook
- ☐ Cancelled checks
- ☐ Savings account statements
- ☐ Tax returns
- ☐ Credit card statements

■ Investments

- ☐ 401(k) statements
- ☐ Roth 401(k) statements
- ☐ CD statements
- ☐ Annuity statements
- ☐ Mutual funds statements
- ☐ IRA statements
- ☐ Stock certificates
- ☐ Bonds
- ☐ Savings bonds

■ Medical

- ☐ Medical records
  (type _____)
- ☐ Medical records
  (type _____)
- ☐ Medical records
  (type _____)
- ☐ Medical records
  (type _____)
- ☐ Medical records
  (type _____)
- ☐ Medical records
  (type _____)
- ☐ Dental records
- ☐ List of medications
- ☐ Advance directive/healthcare proxy

■ Business

- ☐ Corporation paperwork
- ☐ Partnership agreements
- ☐ Business bank statements
- ☐ Business insurance
- ☐ Business tax return

Essential Document Locator

Go back to pages 16 and 17 and list below the items you checked and where they are located. Use the following key: SB (safe deposit box), FB (fireproof box), FC (file cabinet), S (safe), C (computer), O (other_____).

Safe deposit box bank and location	Key location
Fireproof box location	Key location or combination location
File cabinet location	Key location (if locked)
Safe location	Key location or combination location

Document	Location	Document	Location

What I Own

In the first column, list particular assets (this could include homes, vehicles, jewelry, collectibles, collections, etc.). In the second column, list their approximate value as far as you know it. In the third column, list items for which there is still debt outstanding.

Asset	Value	Debts Outstanding

Important Medical Information

Do you know your medical history? Most of us tend not to think about our health until we get a cold, or worse, we experience an unexpected health crisis. Having pertinent information about your medical history at your fingertips could save your life. If for some reason you become incapacitated, this information can guide doctors and nurses in their care for you. Also, when you experience common ailments, this information is beneficial to your physician. So what information do you need to know?

■ Helpful Medical Information

Allergies. List all allergies to foods, medications, and any specific seasonal or indoor allergies you have. This knowledge aids medical staff in their treatment and helps them avoid prescribing medicine that might trigger an allergic reaction.

Doctors' names. Note your primary physician's name and phone number. Record the names of additional physicians you've consulted (for example, specialists) and their contact information as a safety net.

Medications. List the medications and dosages you regularly take, including over-the-counter drugs. Some medications cause reactions when mixed with other drugs. If the medical staff knows what you are currently taking, they can make informed choices in their treatment plan.

Pharmacy information. Provide your pharmacy's name and phone number. Doctors use this information to gain a history of your medications, how often they are filled, and so on.

Medical history. Make a list of your medical and surgical history, such as any chronic medical issues, especially if you are currently undergoing treatment. For your surgical history, be sure to note if you have any artificial devices in your body (pacemakers, hips, implants, etc.). This information can equip your doctor to make life-saving strategies. For instance, if you note that you have pacemaker, your doctor will know that an MRI is not an option for you.

Advance directive. An advance directive is a living will, which includes your medical treatment choices should you become incapacitated and unable to speak for yourself. You can designate a healthcare proxy—the person who will make medical decisions on your behalf. An advance directive can help you explain the types of treatment you want or wish to avoid. (For more information on advance directives, see the article "What Is a Living Will?" on page 44.)

Blood type. Record your blood type. While most medical facilities can quickly type your blood, providing that information up front will speed along treatment.

Insurance. Identify your medical insurance provider and your policy number(s). This will aid you in gaining the necessary preapproval for in-network doctors, treatments, and tests and helps you avoid incurring unnecessary costs.

—Emily White Youree

My Medical Information

Use the following chart to write your medical history. It is very important to keep the information current.

Blood type	
Allergies	
Drug allergies	

Current medications and dosage amounts:

Medication	Dosage Amount	Purpose	Generic OK? Y/N

Physician, pharmacy, and insurance information should be recorded on pages 10 and 11.

My Medical History

Previous medications and dosage amounts:

Medication	Dosage	Purpose	Dates	Prescribing Physician

Previous surgeries:

Surgery	Surgeon	Date	What Was Done?

Do you have any artificial devices implanted? What and when? By whom, if within the last five years?

_____

_____

_____

_____

_____

Chronic medical conditions:

Diagnosis	Treatment

Chronic familial illnesses (heart disease, cancer, osteoporosis, etc.)

Relative	Illness

Choosing Life Insurance

Wondering if life insurance is worth it if your budget is already stretched thin? If you don't have life insurance, how will your family afford all of the expenses that occur in the event of an untimely death? Life insurance ensures that your family finances will remain stable should such an event occur.

There are two basic kinds of policies: *term life* and *whole life*. You'll likely hear about a few other types of life insurance, but they're a variation of one of these two policies. Here's how the two are different.

■ Term Life

Term life insurance is effective for a set period of time; for example, from the date you make the first payment until the predetermined date that the policy ends (typically ten years). Some term policies can extend longer than that, and others are renewable on the anniversary of the policy. Term life insurance is the least expensive, and it pays your beneficiaries only if your death occurs when your policy is in effect. In other words, if you die after your policy expires, your family doesn't get the money you paid in to the policy or the benefit. People buy term insurance because it offers a large amount of benefit for your family for a small monthly payment and can cover just a certain period: when your children are still at home or possibly when you need to care for an aging relative.

■ Whole Life

Whole life insurance covers you for your entire life: from the time you start paying on your policy until the moment you die, as long as the previous payments are continued. And when you die, a whole life policy pays the entire amount to your family. Whole life insurance companies also sell these policies as investment accounts—taking the money paid into the account, investing it, and paying policy holders dividends on those investments while still living.

Many people choose a whole life policy as an investment, hoping that their policy returns big dividends as well as provides for their family after they die. Whole life insurance is often more expensive than term insurance, but it allows for investment potential and security for your dependents.

■ Finding the Right Agent

With insurance agents on just about every corner of every city, finding the right one to represent you can be daunting. Any life insurance company in the US must be licensed by your state. While the state doesn't necessarily rate these companies, you can find information, ratings, and customer reviews about individual insurance companies on the internet (check out www.ambest.com or www.lifeinsure.com to get you started). Ask friends or your employer who they recommend. If you are happy with the insurer that handles your home or car insurance, ask about their policies. Many times you can get a discounted rate for having multiple policies with the same company. Sit down with a few agents and get a feel for their values and worldview. Ask them questions that will give you a good feel for their life perspective, such as:

- » What core values motivate you?
- » What do you invest your time and money in?
- » When you die, what do you want people to remember about you?

Look for someone who shares the same perspective you do. After all, you're making a big investment and trusting his or her recommendations.

After you've found the right agent, ask him or her questions about the policies the company offers. Consider these questions:

- » What kind of life insurance do you have? Why did you choose that policy?
- » What is your company's track record of financial accountability and customer care?

- » What kind of policy do you recommend at my age?
- » How much life insurance do I need?

As you talk to an agent, consider this question: "Who will need financial care and security when I die?" You will need to prepare for estate taxes and any last debts. Also consider the loss of income for your family. You'll want enough insurance to give your family a comfortable living—to pay off the mortgage or ensure that your children have college tuition. Remember, the higher the policy return, the higher your premiums will be.

Buying life insurance is important. Before you spend the money, take the time to talk with several experts in your community. That way you will get the right policy for your needs.

—Tim Baker

What Should Be in a Safe Deposit Box?

Preparedness is an ingredient of the wisdom God offers. Judging by the curves life sometimes throws at you, a certain amount of preparedness ensures peace of mind. While you can never predict a fire or some other emergency, you can take steps to safeguard all of your important documents in case of an emergency. Perhaps you're already secure in the knowledge that your documents are all in one accessible place. But is that location fire- or burglarproof? If not, consider a fireproof safe or a safe deposit box to store the most important documents in your life.

One option is to store these items in a fireproof safe within your home. A safe can cost from $150 to $700 or more. If you've ever lost an important document and have experienced the hassle of procuring a duplicate, you may find that a safe is a good investment.

Another option is a safe deposit box at your local bank. Rental fees are based on the size of the box and can run anywhere from $15 to $25 per year for a small box; $185 to $500 per year for a large box. There is also a key deposit fee of $10 to $15 per year. Check with your bank about applicable fees. You can also deduct the expense of a safe deposit box when you file your income tax if you use the box to store stocks and bonds.

If you choose to have a safe deposit box, record in this book information about how to gain access to it should something happen to you.

Wondering what documents to include in a fireproof safe or safe deposit box? Use the checklist below. If you are missing some important documents, consult the article "Where to Write for Vital Information" at the Centers for Disease Control and Prevention website (http://www.cdc.gov/nchs/w2w .htm) or the Federal Citizen Information Center website (http://www.pueblo.gsa.gov/).

■ Personal Papers

» Copy of your will. While your attorney will have the original copy, more than likely he or she has given you two copies. You can keep one in your safe deposit box.
» Living wills
» Marriage certificate
» Birth or adoption certificate
» Death certificate. If a significant family member has died, you can keep a copy of the death certificate in your box.
» Cemetery deeds along with burial instructions
» Passport
» School diplomas and other education records (transcripts)
» Professional license
» Separation/divorce papers
» Social Security card
» Powers of attorney
» Health information. This includes a record of vaccinations, hospitalizations, and allergy information.
» Military records. Records include dates of tours of duty and discharge papers. Missing records? Consult the National Personnel Records Center, Military Personnel Records (NPRC-MPR) (http:// www.archives.gov/st-louis/military-personnel/).
» Important photographs

■ Property and Insurance

» Deeds or titles for properties and cars
» Other property records (appraisals)
» Homeowner's insurance policy
» Auto insurance policy
» Receipts for home improvements
» Receipts for expensive household items
» Collectibles or rare items. These could include rare coins, stamps, jewelry, and art pieces.
» Home inventory. You can make a room-by-room inventory of your valuables through software found at the Know Your Stuff® Home Inventory website. You might also create a DVD or videotaped inventory.

■ Financials

» Employment contracts
» Original stock certificates
» Bonds and treasury securities
» US savings bonds

—Tom Taylor

Safe Deposit Box Contents

*With many advisors
there is true victory.*

Proverbs 11:14

HOW
to Access
the
Information

*A wise person will listen and continue to learn,
and an understanding person will gain direction.*

Proverbs 1:5

Need to Know

Identity Theft: Protect Yourself

Need to Know

This page gives you a place to record basic access information to your accounts. Also use this page to record your credit card information in case you should ever lose your credit cards.

■ Bank and Credit Union Accounts

Bank Name	Account Number	PIN	Type of Account

■ Credit/Debit Cards

Company	Account Number	PIN	Toll-Free Phone Number

■ Insurance Policies

Type	Company	Policy Number	Phone Number

■ Website Information

Site	User Name	Password

Identity Theft: Protect Yourself

In recent years, identity theft has become a major issue throughout the United States. About nine million people are the victims of identity theft each year. But you can reduce your risk of identity theft by following a few simple guidelines.

■ Ask Questions

Talk to your bank about what they are doing to ward off identity theft. Find out from your credit card company if you will be liable for any fraudulent charges. Ask your employer about what they do to safeguard your important employee information.

■ Shred Sensitive Documents

Bank deposit receipts, credit card statements, and old documents contain sensitive information. If you no longer need this information, consider shredding these documents rather than throwing them away. Criminals can learn a lot of information from digging through garbage.

■ Shop at Secure Websites

Online shopping is a great tool. Not all sites, however, are safe. One way to tell that a web page is secure is to look at the bottom or top of your browser for a graphic that looks like a lock. Another way is the "https" in the address bar. This https stands for "hypertext transfer protocol secure." This shows that you are on a secure web page and the data transferred over is encrypted. Without this secure connection, hackers are able to sift through your transaction and steal your personal information.

■ Don't Become "Phish" Food

Phishing is an online scam. Hackers claiming to represent reputable companies (phone companies, banks, credit card companies, even government agencies) send email or instant messages to gain sensitive information (passwords, social security numbers, or other account information). These messages might contain a link for you to click on or ask you to double-check or provide sensitive personal information. Responsible organizations *never* ask for sensitive information by email. Don't be fooled!

■ Don't Fall for Telephone Scams

Avoid giving out your personal information to someone who initiates contact with you by telephone and claims to represent a bank, credit card company, charity, or other organization. Always verify the credentials before giving out your information.

■ Use Antiviral Software and Pop-Up Blockers

Viruses and Trojans craftily find their way into your computer through your internet downloads and can compromise your private information. Viruses attach themselves to documents or files that are spread when you share or receive and open files; Trojans appear to be useful software, but they do damage to your computer if you download and run them. You can combat this by updating your anti-virus program and subscribing to advertising pop-up blockers. Another good habit to get into is to regularly delete your internet history and browser cookies.

■ Check Your Credit Report

The United States law grants all Americans one free credit report each year. You can get the free report from the three major credit agencies by going to www.annualcreditreport.com. Check to make sure that all the information is correct and check for any strange activity. If you disagree with any of the information, you can work with the credit company to make changes. Check their websites for how to resolve disputes.

■ Secure Your Important Documents

Your birth certificate, Social Security card, passport, and other identifying documents are extremely important. Take care that these documents are safely stored away. (See "What Should Be in a Safe Deposit Box?" on page 25.) If you can, avoid carrying these documents around with you. While traveling abroad, secure your passport by leaving it in a hotel room safe.

■ Social Security Numbers Are Very Important

Many insurance companies and colleges use customers' Social Security numbers as a way of identifying you. This method gives this number far too much exposure. Since a Social Security number can easily be used to obtain a vast amount of private information about you, ask these institutions not to use this number to identify you in their system; rather, have them substitute a different number instead.

■ Be Wise on Social Networks

Over four hundred million people use social networks like Facebook to keep in touch. Sadly, hackers also use these sites to gain new victims. Consider limiting the amount of personal information you include in your profile on these sites.

If your identity has been stolen, file a police report, check your credit report, and contact your bank and credit card company.

—Tom Taylor

WHEN
I'm Not Here

Teach us to number each of our days so that we may grow in wisdom.

Psalm 90:12

What My Family Can Expect

at the Funeral Home

My Groups and Organizations

My Autobiography

My Funeral and Burial Requests

What Should Be in My Will?

Gifts

What Is a Living Will?

What My Family Can Expect at the Funeral Home

One of the most difficult aspects a family faces after the death of a loved one is the immediate need to make burial and funeral arrangements. In such a time of grief, making choices can seem overwhelming.

The funeral director can offer sympathetic support for the grieving family members while overseeing many of the preparations for the burial. Since there is usually only a two- to four-day window in which to make arrangements, the funeral director is a welcome and efficient guide through this process.

The following checklist provides some of the details a family can expect when meeting with a funeral director. And here is where you can help. You can make the process easier by dictating these decisions now, using the forms on the following pages.

■ Burial or Cremation

» **Prepurchased cemetery plot.** If a plot has been purchased previously, the family should bring the deed with them when meeting with the funeral director. Or the family will be able to purchase one during the time they meet with the funeral director.

» **Casket and container.** The funeral director will work with the family on the options for a casket (wood, metal, fiberglass, fiberboard) or a burial container. A burial container keeps the ground around a casket from caving in. There are two options: a vault or a grave liner. A grave liner only covers the top and sides of a casket in concrete. A vault ensures that the whole casket is surrounded in concrete; therefore, it is more expensive.

» **Mausoleum.** A mausoleum is an aboveground structure that houses the remains. A mausoleum can be public or private.

» **Cremation.** If cremation is chosen, a container will be selected (wood, bronze, copper, biodegradable, keepsake).

■ Preparing/Embalming the Body

» **Preparing.** What clothing or jewelry will the deceased person wear during the viewing and funeral? The funeral director needs to know if any of the jewelry should be removed and given to the family before burial.

» **Embalming.** Embalming, in most cases, is only required if the body is to be viewed at the funeral or during viewing hours. If the family has chosen to have the body cremated, they may be asked to identify the body prior to the funeral, whether or not they planned on having a viewing. They may want to consider whether embalming would be helpful so that the last image of their loved one looks more like the person they knew them to be. If the family chooses embalming, they should be sure to provide the funeral director with a photo of their loved one.

■ Death Certificate and Obituary

» **Death certificate.** The funeral director will obtain the death certificate(s). It is a good practice for the family to order more than they think they'll need, as death certificates may later be required for any number of reasons.

» **Obituary.** The family will need to decide what newspaper(s) will carry the obituary. Some newspapers will run a death notice without charge, but most charge for an obituary. The funeral director will walk the family through the essential information to include and what is optional for the obituary. The funeral director will usually place the finished obituary in the newspapers, but families should confirm this.

◼ Eulogy

» The funeral director will offer guidance for choosing clergy or a friend to deliver the eulogy. The eulogy can be developed by expanding on the obituary and making it more personal. The funeral director can give suggestions for content of the eulogy.

◼ Funeral Service

» **Questions about the service.** The funeral director can help the family decide when the funeral will be held—before or after burial or cremation—and whether to hold a graveside service. (The funeral can be after a graveside service even if the casket is not present.) The director can offer advice about the order of service and what options the funeral home offers.

» **Flowers.** Families will be asked their preference on the display of arrangements at the visitation/viewing, funeral, and/or graveside services. The funeral director can suggest options.

» **Photos or portraits.** Photos of the deceased can be made available at the service for family and friends to peruse.

» **Pallbearers.** The family will need to choose four to six men. Since pallbearers are not usually immediate family members, they might ask friends and extended family members.

» **Costs.** The deceased may have life insurance or a previously purchased plan to pay for funeral expenses. If not, family members can elect to split the expenses. Many funeral homes also allow monthly payments to be made over a period of three or more years.

—Sharon Kaufman

My Groups and Organizations

In the event of your passing, your loved ones will want to pass along the information to those who know and love you. List these organizations and contact or website information below.

Alumni Associations

School Name	My Graduation Year	Website

Civic Organizations

Organization Name	My Involvement	Website

Clubs

Club Name	My Involvement	Website

Church and Military Organizations

Organization Name	My Involvement	Website

Other

Organization Name	My Involvement	Website

*Everlasting life is on the way
of righteousness.*

Proverbs 12:28

My Autobiography

You don't need to write an entire autobiography, but you know better than anyone what you hope to be remembered for. Help your loved ones to create a meaningful obituary by giving some basic information below. Write about your family, some important accomplishments, your interests and hobbies, etc.

My Funeral and Burial Requests

On this page, help your loved ones in a time of grief by giving information about any preplanning you have already done (perhaps you already have a burial plot or have prepaid some funeral expenses) and your wishes.

Preferred or selected funeral home:

_____

Burial plot information:

_____

_____

Preferred pastor:

_____

Desired location of funeral service:

_____

_____

Wishes for my body and my burial:

_____

Chosen executor:

_____

Prearrangements I have completed:

_____

_____

_____

_____

Favorite hymns or songs:

_____

_____

_____

_____

Favorite Bible passages or other readings:

_____

_____

_____

_____

_____

Features that I want my family to include in my funeral:

_____

_____

_____

_____

_____

Other information and requests:

_____

_____

_____

_____

_____

*Good people leave an inheritance to
their grandchildren, but the wealth
of sinners is stored away
for a righteous person.*

Proverbs 13:22

What Should Be in My Will?

Few subjects are more uncomfortable than death. We don't like to think about our lives ending. However, writing a will ensures that even something as uncomfortable as death can be handled with great care.

In its most basic form, a will is a document that describes what you want to happen to your estate: all of your worldly possessions including your house, clothes, car, children, and anything else that belongs to you. Once you die and all of your debts (taxes, death duties, and other liabilities) are satisfied, your will goes into effect, and your estate is divided according to your wishes.

Ways to Write a Will

Well-known will phrases like *This is my last will and testament* and *I, John Smith, being of sound mind and body* that you've heard in movies or read in books aren't clichés. They're actually important introductions for a will. These statements assure the judge and your executor that you are thinking clearly, that your will can be trusted, and that you mean what you say. That's key for a legal document outlining your final wishes.

There are a few different ways to create a will. You can write it yourself, you can use a computer program or download a form from the internet, or you can hire a lawyer. Each of these methods has strengths. If you create your own document, you save the expense of a lawyer. If you have a lawyer write your will for you, you get the benefit of an expert. Keep in mind the fee for writing a will starts at around $100 for a simple will and increases if you have a large estate.

Whichever method you use, your will needs to be witnessed by two or three close friends. They should watch you sign the will, and they should also sign their names to attest to the validity of the document. While it's not necessary to have your will notarized, most experts recommend doing so in case your will is disputed after your death. Your will should be kept in a secure place, such as your home safe or a safe deposit box at your bank. (For more information on where to keep a will, see the article "What Should Be in a Safe Deposit Box?" on page 25.)

Your Executor

An executor is the person charged with handling your estate. This person makes sure that your property goes to the people you designate in your will. This person also makes sure that all of your final bills are paid and that your children are delivered to their guardian. An executor is your voice.

If you're married and don't have a will, the court will likely appoint your spouse as your executor. If you're not married, think carefully about the person you choose who will serve in this capacity. Many people choose a close family friend, one of their grown children, or some other trustworthy person. Prayerfully consider who will be your executor. Your executor, lawyer, spouse, and any other close family member should have a copy of your will and know where the original is kept.

■ Your Beneficiaries

The people you name in your will are your beneficiaries. If you are married, your spouse is the most obvious person to include in your will. In most states, all of your possessions automatically go to your spouse when you die. Still, if you want to designate anything specific about those possessions (for example, you'd like your spouse to get everything, but you'd like your twenty-one-year-old son to get your 1978 Pontiac Firebird), you will need to state this in your will.

If you have children, you'll need to designate how much of your estate you want to go to each child. If you have certain possessions you feel would be best suited for one specific child, state that in your will. You should also designate someone to serve as the legal guardian of your children in the event that both you and your spouse die. This person must be willing and able to serve in this capacity. If you have several close family members, ask one to serve as the guardian over your children, and the other to serve as the trustee of the estate your children inherit. This provides a built-in system of checks and balances and prevents one family member from controlling your estate.

Outlining where you want your possessions to go is especially important if your spouse is deceased or you are unmarried. If you are married, your will should include the following phrasing: *In the event of my spouse's death, I want my possessions to be divided up between my children in the following ways.*

Your parents, your best friend, and your favorite charities can also be included as beneficiaries if you'd like any of your possessions to go to them.

—Tim Baker

Gifts

Use this page to write down items that you want to give to specific people or organizations—items too small to be included in the will. For example, a certain tablecloth to a daughter-in-law who always admired it, or a certain book to a specific grandchild.

Item	Location	Person/Group I Want to Receive It

■ Other Wishes

_____

_____

_____

What Is a Living Will?

A living will is different from a last will and testament. A last will and testament is a legal document outlining what you want to happen to your body and possessions after your death. A living will outlines your wishes if you're critically incapacitated and therefore unable to voice those wishes. A living will goes into effect when you need medical support to sustain life (life-supporting systems, lifesaving medications). Because doctors have taken an oath to protect life, they will do everything medically possible in an emergency. Yet they still require permission in regard to life support.

These days, the term "living will" isn't used as much as the term "advance directive." If you've ever checked in to a hospital, you may have seen the latter. There are two types of advance directives: a living will and a healthcare power of attorney. The first outlines the medical treatment choices you would like carried out should you become incapacitated and unable to voice these choices. The second gives power of attorney in regard to medical treatment to a designated person—a healthcare proxy.

Each type of advance directive answers the following questions:

» If you're unable to sustain life on your own, do you want the doctors to keep you alive?
» If your heart fails while you're in the care of the hospital staff, do you want them to resuscitate you? If yes, how many times?
» What other life-sustaining care are you willing to receive if you're incapacitated (for example, cardiopulmonary resuscitation, hospice care)?
» What medical care do you wish to avoid?

These are big questions. You might consult a pastor and a lawyer to make sure you understand all of the implications of your decisions.

■ Healthcare Proxy

A healthcare proxy (or patient advocate) is the person you've legally designated to make all of your healthcare decisions when you can't speak for yourself. He or she has to be over the age of eighteen. This person can be a spouse, a sibling, your adult child, or a trusted friend. If you have a living will, this person will ensure that your wishes in that document are carried out. If you don't have any documentation about the kind of treatment you desire, this person can still act on your behalf.

You can download a healthcare proxy form from the internet. Since regulations may vary from state to state, be sure you know the requirements for your state.

■ Drafting a Living Will

Most experts recommend that you have an attorney draft your living will because an attorney knows the correct legal language to use. However, you can draft your own living will. As with any official document, a living will should be signed by you, and its signing should be witnessed by two or three close friends or relatives. You can also have it notarized. Keep the document in a safe place and give a copy to the person you trust to act on your behalf in the event that you are unconscious. (For more information on where to keep a living will, see the article "What Should Be in a Safe Deposit Box?" on page 25.)

Appendix

Great treasure is in the house
of a righteous person.

Proverbs 15:6

Recommended Reading

Helpful Websites

Recommended Reading

The 25-Day Money Makeover for Women, Francine L. Huff (Revell, 2006).

The Alpha Last Will and Testament Kit: Special Book Edition with Removable Forms, Kermit Burton (Alpha Publications of America, 1998).

Family Tree Legacies: Preserving Memories Throughout Time, Allison Stacy and Diane Haddad (Family Tree Books, 2009).

Glimpses of Heaven, Trudy Harris (Revell, 2008).

Grave Matters: A Journey Through the Modern Funeral Industry to a Natural Way of Burial, Mark Harris (Scribner, 2008).

The Household Money Organizer, Baker Publishing Group (Revell, 2010).

Our Family Tree, Julie Hausner (Book Sales, 2000).

Stopping Identity Theft: 10 Easy Steps to Security, Scott Mitic (NOLO, 2009).

Organizing for Life, Sandra Felton (Revell, 2007).

Helpful Websites

■ Wills and Other Documents

Crown Financial Ministries, www.crown.org (visit the library of articles on "Wills and Trusts")

Legal Zoom (legal documents), www.legalzoom.com

■ Identity Theft

Federal Trade Commission/Fighting Back Against Identity Theft, www.ftc.gov/bcp/edu/microsites/idtheft

U.S. Department of Justice/Fraud Section, www.justice.gov/criminal/fraud/websites/idtheft.html

Identity Theft Resource Center, www.idtheftcenter.org

■ Safe Deposit Boxes

All Financial Matters, allfinancialmatters.com/2006/06/25/what-belongs-in-your-safe-deposit-box

eHow, www.ehow.com/list_5994454_items-keep-safe-deposit-box.html

■ End-of-Life Issues

Local funeral homes often have helpful information on their individual websites.

Some issues vary from state to state, so be sure to check the information that applies to your state.

Hospice Foundation of America, www.hospicefoundation.org

National Library of Medicine/National Institutes of Health, www.nlm.nih.gov/medlineplus/endoflifeissues.html

Funeralwise.com, http://www.funeralwise.com/plan/ceremony

National Center on Caregiving/Family Caregiver Alliance, www.caregiver.org